MY FIRST BOOK of NATURE

Camilla
de la Bedoyere

Jane
Newland

templar
books

CONTENTS

Plants

Bugs

LADYBIRD HUNT

Can you find the ladybirds
hiding in this book? There is one
in every scene, all except one.

Go to page 63 to find out.

MY FIRST BOOK of NATURE

A TEMPLAR BOOK

THIS EDITION PUBLISHED IN THE UK IN 2020 BY TEMPLAR BOOKS.
FIRST PUBLISHED IN THE UK IN 2018 BY TEMPLAR BOOKS,
AN IMPRINT OF BONNIER BOOKS UK,
THE PLAZA, 535 KING'S ROAD, LONDON, SW10 0SZ
WWW.TEMPLARCO.CO.UK
WWW.BONNIERBOOKS.CO.UK

1 3 5 7 9 10 8 6 4 2

ISBN 978-1-78741-714-4

WRITTEN BY CAMILLA DE LA BEDOYERE
DESIGNED BY OLIVIA COOK
EDITED BY CARLY BLAKE AND SAMUEL FERN
CONSULTED BY SEAN CALLERY

PRINTED IN CHINA

Birds

Animals

Plants

Oak

Sweet pea

Rose

Bird of paradise flower

Pitcher plant

Dandelion

Cactus

Scots pine

Apple blossom

Vine

Sunflower

Palm

Giant sequoia

Fern

Orchid

Daisy

THE STORY OF A SEED

A seed holds new life inside, and with warmth, air and water it can grow into a new plant. This is how a broad bean plant grows from a little seed.

Plants need sunlight to grow

Corn kernel

Sycamore seed

Avocado stone

Seeds can be tiny or as big as your head. Many are round, some are flat and others have wings.

Burr

Mountain laurel seed

Poppy seeds

(4) More and more leaves shoot out as the plant grows tall and strong.

(3) A green shoot grows up towards the light. Two little leaves unfurl and open.

(2) The seed's case cracks open and a white root grows down. It sucks up water from the soil.

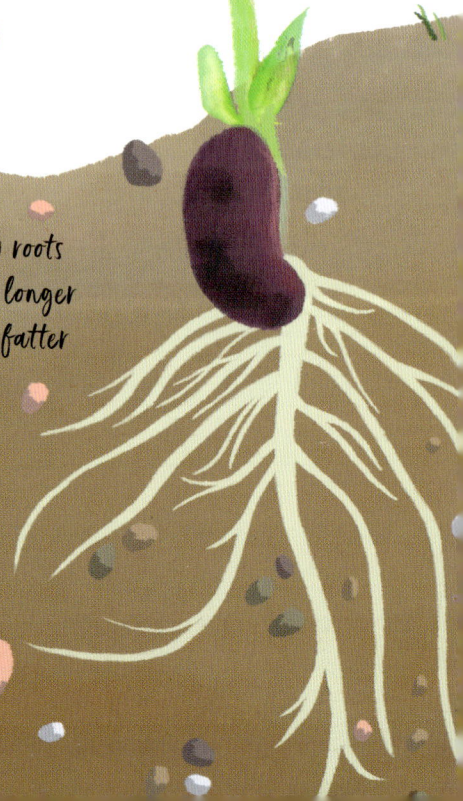

New roots grow longer and fatter

First root

(1) A seed falls onto the ground or it is buried.

It's damp and dark in the soil

Broad bean plant

Growing plants need plenty of water

⑤
Flower buds appear, and burst into colourful petals.

Purple flowers

Hungry snails munch on the sweet juicy leaves of young plants

The plant's roots keep on growing. They hold the seedling in the ground so it doesn't fall over.

9

ALL ABOUT FLOWERS

A huge golden sunflower lifts its face to the sun and shows off its petals. It has an important job to do and it needs the help of some buzzing bees. Flowers make seeds.

(1) The sunflower's sweet smell and yellow petals attract bees.

A sunflower head has lots of tiny flowers in its centre

(2) A bee sips the sugary nectar inside the flower and brushes against a yellow powder called pollen.

(3) The bee flies from flower to flower looking for nectar to drink.

Most plants have flowers, and many of them are big and colourful with a sweet smell.

Rose

Daffodil

Daisy

(5)

Now, the sunflower begins to change. Each tiny flower grows into a seed.

A goldfinch perches on the sunflower to eat the tasty seeds

(4)

When the bee lands on another flower, some pollen falls off. This is called pollination.

Foxglove

Pollen dust sticks to a bee's furry body

Lily

Passionflower

11

NATURE'S HARVEST

Fruits and vegetables grow in all sorts of shapes, sizes and colours. Some vegetables are hidden underground, but many fruits grow high up in the trees. They are food for lots of animals – including us!

A vegetable is any part of a plant that is good to eat, from leafy green shoots to plump roots.

This pea pod has just popped!

Peas and beans grow inside a pod. When the pod pops open, they are scattered around and will grow in new places.

Carrots, potatoes, yams and beets are some of the vegetables that grow in the soil, or just at its surface.

Radish

Beetroot

Lettuce

A carrot is a thick orange root

Potatoes

These vegetables are ready to be dug up!

Oranges, lemons, limes and grapefruits are citrus fruits. They have thick skin and juicy insides high in vitamin C.

Lemons

Bananas grow in bunches

A fruit is the part of a plant that grows around a seed. As fruits ripen in the hot summer sun, they grow sweeter.

Grapes are berries

A berry is a fruit with seeds inside. A tomato is a berry with lots of seeds, but a cranberry has just four.

Tropical fruits, such as bananas and pineapples, grow in hot places where there is sunshine and rain all year round.

A pumpkin is a type of vegetable called a squash

Rambutans

Pink dragon fruit

Pineapple

BEWARE!
Some fruits and vegetables must be cooked before they are eaten. Never eat any part of a plant unless an adult tells you it's safe.

13

TOWERING TREES

Trees grow tall and strong, raising their leaves high into the sky where the sun shines brightest. They can be found all over the world, except where it's very cold or very hot.

Oak tree in winter

Oak tree in summer

Scots pine

When summer ends, broadleaf trees such as oaks drop their leaves. In spring, they will burst into life again.

Acorns

Pine cones

Larches are conifers, but their needles change colour and fall in the autumn

Tall, spindly conifer trees, like Scots pines, grow in cool places. They keep their needle-like leaves all year, and their seeds grow in cones.

One tree ring shows one year of growth. How old do you think this tree is?

The Cedar of Lebanon is sturdy and stout with wide-reaching branches. It grows on steep mountainsides and can live for hundreds of years.

Cedar of Lebanon

Baobab tree

Tall baobabs are called upside-down trees! When it rains they store the water in their fat trunks.

Coconut palm

Conifer trees are also called evergreens

Mango tree

A palm tree unfurls its big leafy fronds from the top of its trunk. Tree ferns look like small palm trees.

Tree fern

The branches of fruit trees may bend and droop, but they are strong enough to hold hundreds of plump fruits.

Mango fruit

ALL KINDS OF LEAVES

From prickly cactus spines to huge fan-shaped fronds, leaves are working hard all the time. A leaf is the place where a plant makes its food.

Needle-shaped

Most leaves are broad and flat, so they can catch lots of sunlight. They come in many different shapes, but there are five main types.

Lots of animals eat leaves as food. Clever orangutans use them to build nests and to scoop up water to drink.

Big leaves can be useful as umbrellas for orangutans!

Barrel cactus

Oval-shaped

Long

Hand-shaped

Compound
(many leaves on one stem)

Plants make food in a special
way called photosynthesis
(foh-toh-sin-the-sis).

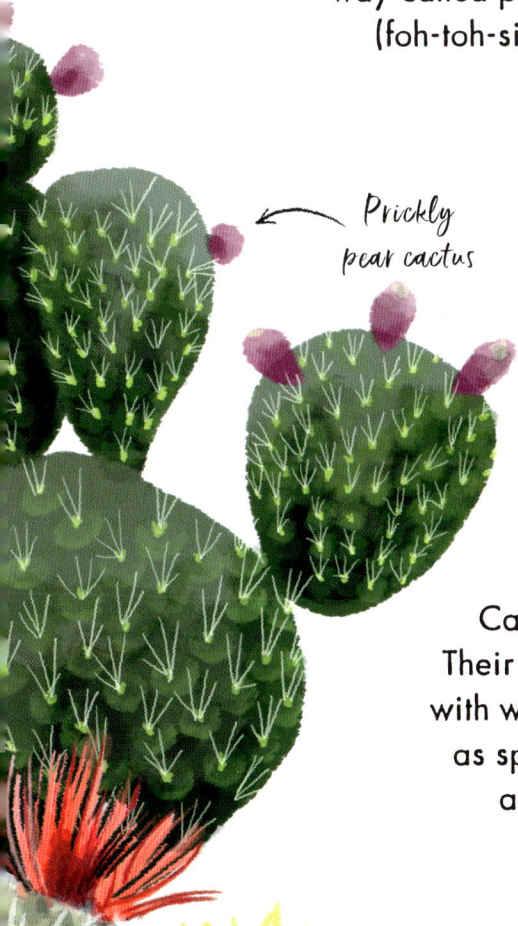

(2) Air is sucked into leaves through
tiny holes in their surface

(1) Sunlight passes
into leaves

Prickly
pear cactus

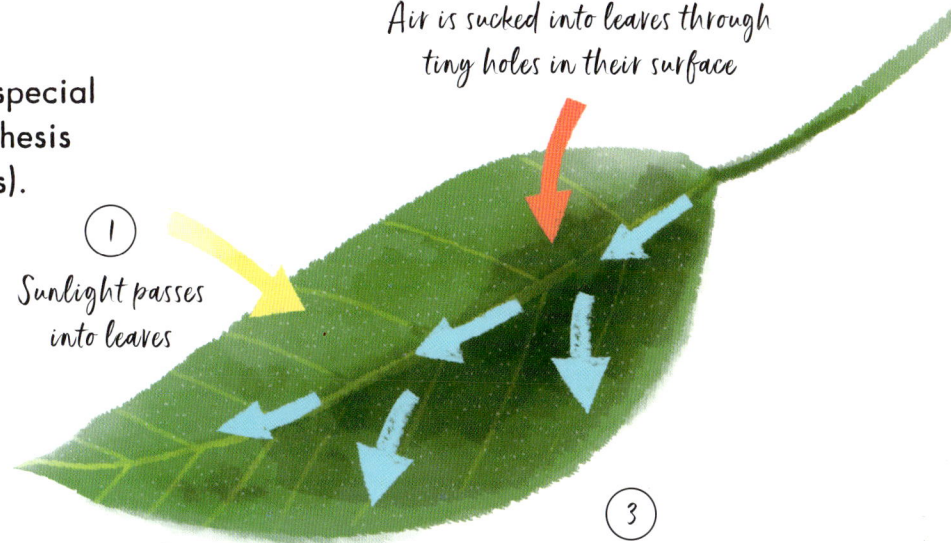

(3) Water travels from the soil into the
roots, up the stem to the leaves

(4) Leaves use sunlight to turn
the air and water into food

Cacti grow in hot deserts.
Their stems are fat and swollen
with water and their leaves grow
as spines. These prickles stop
animals nibbling them!

Rabbits eat juicy
grass stems

The thick, flat leaves of a
stone plant look like pebbles

THE RAINFOREST

A rainforest is full of lush, big-leaved plants and towering trees. It rains most days, but it is always hot. Plants like warmth and water, so it's a perfect place for them to grow.

Tree branches create a thick layer of leaves called the canopy

Titan arum and rafflesia (raf-lee-see-a) are huge stinky flowers that grow on the forest floor. Their bad smell attracts flies and other insects.

The long stems of vines dangle from branches

The titan arum's flower is taller than a person!

Below the canopy, palms, ferns, bushes and young trees fight for sunlight

Rafflesia flowers grow to one metre across

Animals, from tigers and hanging sloths to ants and tiny hummingbirds, make their homes in rainforests.

The tallest trees poke out above the canopy

A hummingbird hovers to sip a flower's sweet nectar

Lobster claw flower

Orchid

Some flowers don't need soil at all. Plants like this orchid grow high up on tree branches. Their roots dangle in the damp air.

Colourful mushrooms grow on the ground, where it's gloomy and wet.

Mushrooms

Bugs

Garden spider

Painted lady caterpillar

Painted lady butterfly

Earthworm

Stag beetle

Bumblebee

Crane fly

Aphids

Crab spider

Centipede

Emperor dragonfly

Orchid mantis

Woodlouse

Cuckoo wasp

Black ants

Shield bug

Garden snail

Blow fly

Ladybird

Bella moth

Short-horned grasshopper

Scarab beetle

Stick insect

Bella moth caterpillar

BUG FIGHT!

It's a bug-eat-bug world out there. When bugs are not hunting for food, they're being hunted as food! These crawly critters have some clever ways to catch a meal and avoid attack.

A hornet gives a nasty sting

Yellow and black stripes warn of danger. Most stripy bugs have a sting in their tail.

Many-legged centipedes and speedy tiger beetles can run fast to chase down prey

An army of driver ants is on the march. They work as a team to attack other animals. Big ants, called soldiers, guard the smaller workers.

Soldier ants have large mouthparts to grab and bite

Assassin bugs inject a liquid that turns other bugs to juice!

Orchid mantis

An orchid mantis looks like a pink flower. When another bug comes near it will shoot its spiny front legs forwards in a split-second to grab its meal.

Blackbird

Monarch caterpillars munch on milkweed leaves so that they taste bad to hungry birds

A harmless hoverfly looks like a stinging bug

All of these bugs are masters of trickery. They stay out of danger by pretending to be something else.

A thorn bug pretends to be a prickly thorn

Spicebush swallowtail caterpillars look like mini snakes

A katydid may lose a leg in a fight so it can get away

Click beetles can flick their bodies high into the air

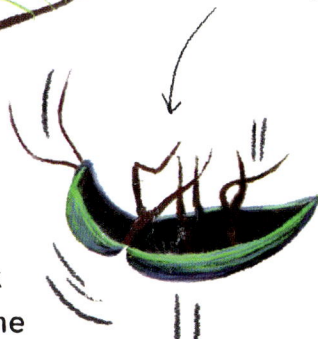

Grasshoppers and click beetles both have the same idea when escaping danger – to jump up and away.

Grasshoppers have long, springy legs for leaping to safety

Bombardier beetle

Beware a fearsome bombardier beetle – it defends itself by spraying a stinging liquid from its bottom!

23

A TIME TO CHANGE

Caterpillars are baby bugs that look very different from the moths and butterflies they change into. This is the life cycle of the monarch butterfly.

When caterpillars turn into butterflies they go through a big change called a metamorphosis (meta-morf-o-sis).

④ The caterpillar makes a hard case, called a chrysalis (kris-uh-lis), around its body.

③ Caterpillars eat and eat and eat! They need to grow fat before they can change.

The caterpillar's stripy skin warns birds that it is poisonous

Chrysalis

② The eggs hatch and little caterpillars appear.

Eggs

① A female butterfly lays her tiny eggs on the underside of a leaf, where birds can't see them.

These baby bugs, or larvae, turn into three very different insects:

Garden tiger caterpillar

Ladybird larva

Honeybee larva

Garden tiger moth

Honeybee

Ladybird

5

Inside the chrysalis, the caterpillar's body turns into a soupy liquid before it takes shape as an adult butterfly.

6

The chrysalis cracks open and a butterfly steps out. It dries its wings in the sun before it can fly away.

Monarch butterfly

7

A male and a female dance in the air before they mate. Then the female is ready to lay her eggs and the story starts again.

I SPY A SPIDER

Most bugs have six legs, but spiders have eight. They can run speedily, build traps and spin silken webs. They are the superheroes of the bug world.

Spinnerets, where silk is made

Spiders hunt other bugs to eat. They have strong jaws and sharp fangs to bite and inject deadly venom.

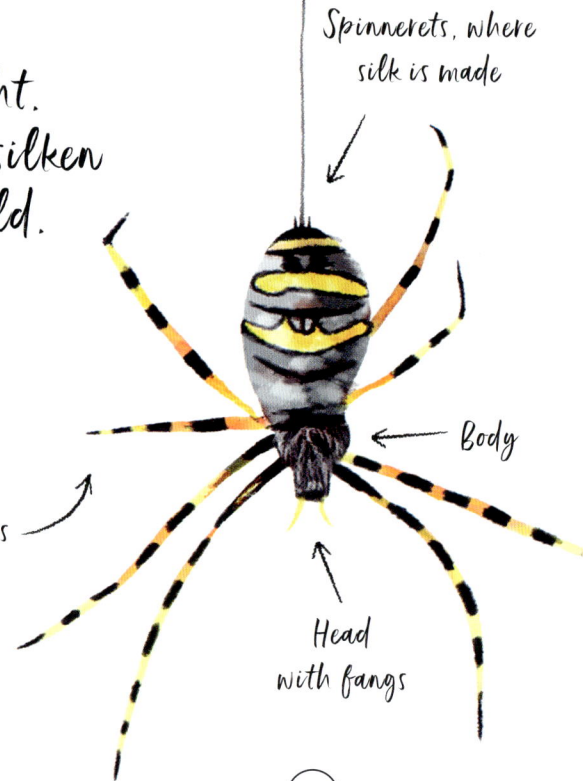

Eight legs

Body

Head with fangs

① A spider spins silk in a Y-shape between twigs, to make a frame.

② Strong silk threads are added to the edges.

③ A sticky silk is used to spin a spiral, starting from the middle.

Fly

④ Hiding close by, a spider waits for a bug to fly into its web.

Many spiders build webs from silk that they make in their spinnerets. They use webs to trap food.

Spiders have huge brains for their body size, and some clever abilities, too. Spiders have super sight – they can have up to 12 eyes, and super senses – they can smell, hear and taste with their feet!

Desert spiders get around by cartwheeling, so their feet don't get burnt on the hot sand

Supermum wolf spiders carry hundreds of babies on their back to keep them safe

The colourful peacock spider can jump high into the air

Trapdoor spiders build a silk door over their burrow entrance, then cover it with soil to make the trap almost invisible.

A net-casting spider hangs on a thread. It holds a stretchy web in its legs, ready to catch a woodlouse!

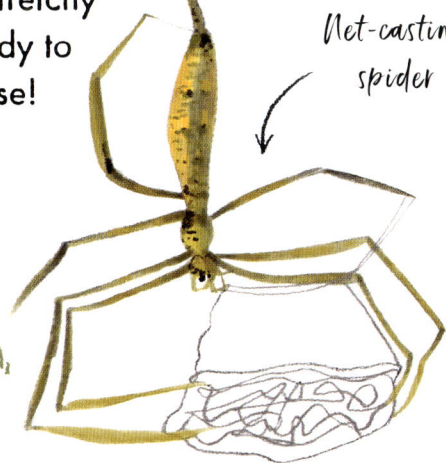

Net-casting spider

Trapdoor spider

POND BUGS

Beneath the shimmering surface of ponds and rivers there is a hidden underwater world of bugs. Here, they can find a home, food and plenty of places to hide.

Adult mayflies live for just a few days

A blue and green emperor dragonfly darts about above a pond. It started its life in the water.

Emperor dragonfly

④ A nymph moults up to 10 times before it climbs out of the water and becomes an adult.

① A dragonfly lays her eggs at the water's surface and sticks them to a plant stem.

Nymphs can spend up to five years underwater

③ As a nymph grows it sheds its old skin. This is called moulting.

② After a few weeks the eggs hatch into tiny, wriggly babies called nymphs.

Frogs lay hundreds of soft eggs, called frogspawn, in the water

Frogspawn

Pond worms can breathe underwater

28

A kingfisher will perch on a branch to look for fish before diving into the water

Crane fly

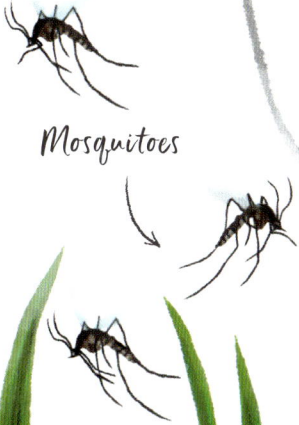

Mosquitoes

Pond skaters scoot along the water's surface. Water boatmen are beetles that swim, using oar-shaped legs to paddle themselves around.

Mosquito larvae hang upside-down from the surface and breathe through their bottoms!

Pond skater

Whirligig beetles can dive to esacpe danger

This diving beetle has a clever way of breathing when it dives. It collects a bubble of air at the surface and carries it down, where it searches for food.

Water boatman

Diving beetle

Water snail

Shrimp

Caddisfly larvae make tough cases around their bodies, covered with tiny rocks and leaves

GOING UNDERGROUND

Millions of bugs are busy beneath our feet.
They lurk under stones, tunnel through soft soil
and munch through piles of old, rotting leaves.

Anteaters use their long sticky tongues to eat their favourite food – ants!

Ants store dead leaves and eat the mould that grows on them

It's all action in an ant nest! Thousands of tiny bugs scurry along tunnels, carrying food, eggs and leaves to different rooms, called chambers.

Worm cast

Seed chamber

Ant graveyard

Earthworm

Worker ants dig new tunnels and chambers

Larvae chamber

Centipedes and millipedes have long, thin bodies – perfect for tunnelling

Only the queen ant lays eggs

Pupae chamber

Earthworms eat soil as they burrow through it

Egg chamber

Centipede

A tunnel is a safe place for worms and other creepy-crawlies to hide out. It's damp and cool and there is always something to eat.

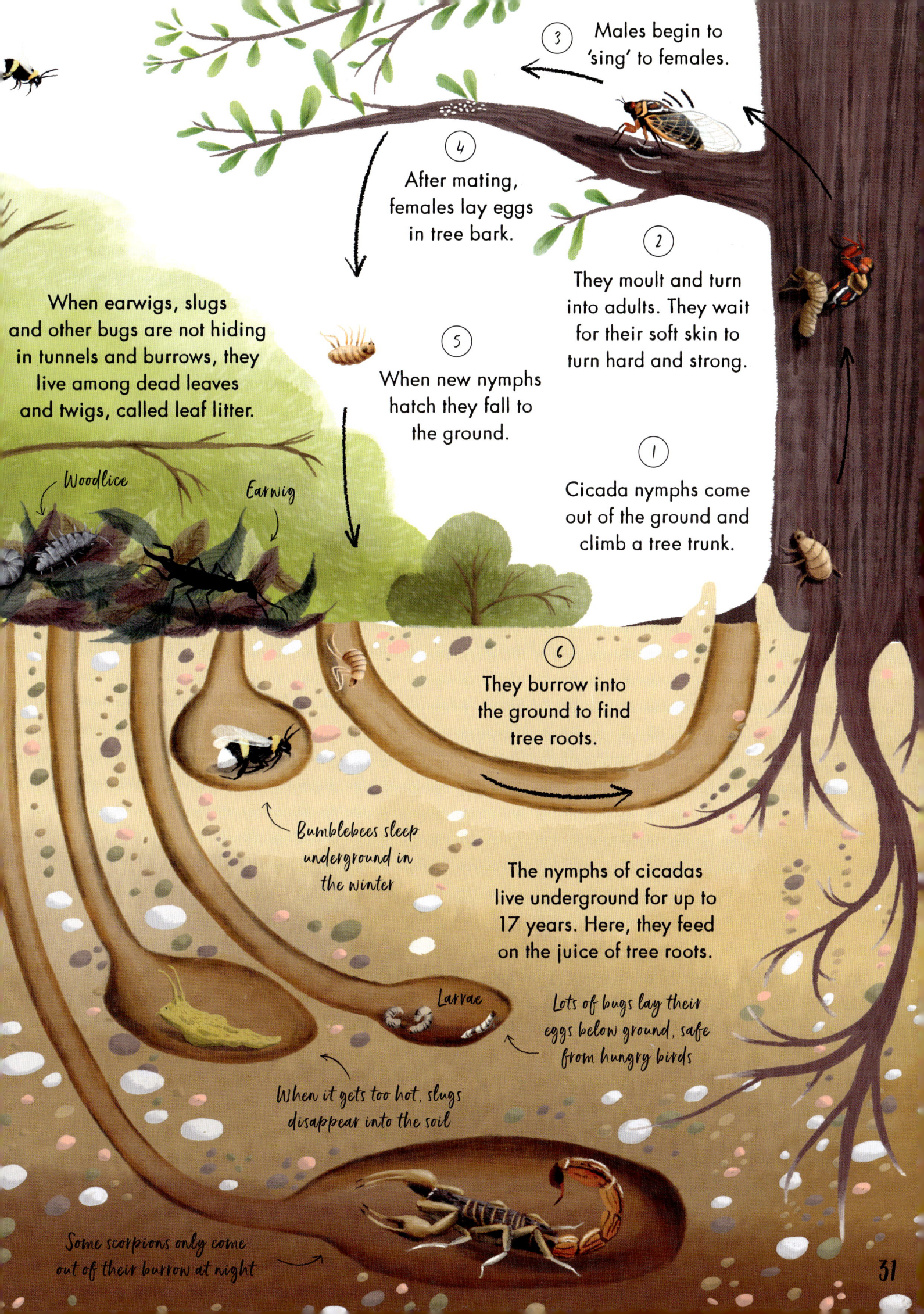

③ Males begin to 'sing' to females.

④ After mating, females lay eggs in tree bark.

② They moult and turn into adults. They wait for their soft skin to turn hard and strong.

⑤ When new nymphs hatch they fall to the ground.

① Cicada nymphs come out of the ground and climb a tree trunk.

When earwigs, slugs and other bugs are not hiding in tunnels and burrows, they live among dead leaves and twigs, called leaf litter.

Woodlice

Earwig

⑥ They burrow into the ground to find tree roots.

Bumblebees sleep underground in the winter

The nymphs of cicadas live underground for up to 17 years. Here, they feed on the juice of tree roots.

Larvae

Lots of bugs lay their eggs below ground, safe from hungry birds

When it gets too hot, slugs disappear into the soil

Some scorpions only come out of their burrow at night

31

BIG BUGS

Meet the incredible creepy-crawlies that hold the record for being the longest, heaviest or biggest. These are supersized bugs!

Tarantula hawk wasp

The weta is a plant-eating monster bug that looks like a plump grasshopper. The biggest wetas are some of the heaviest insects in the world.

A giant weta weighs about the same as an apple

Tarantula hawk wasps measure up to 5 centimetres long but they can defeat tarantulas the size of dinner plates!

The goliath beetle's flying wings are covered by a hard red wing case

The goliath beetle is the world's biggest insect at 11.5 centimetres long. This big bug is so strong it can lift more than 850 times its own weight!

Queen Alexandra's birdwing is the world's largest butterfly, with a wingspan as big as a football. Males have bright green and blue wings.

Queen Alexandra's birdwing butterfly

Chan's megastick

A stick insect looks like a stick! This is Chan's megastick and it can reach 35 centimetres in length.

Huge atlas moths live for just a few weeks. During the day they rest, but when the sun sets they flutter through the rainforest to find a mate.

The Atlas moth is as big as Queen Alexandra's birdwing butterfly

The Amazonian giant centipede only comes out of its burrow to hunt for a meal. It grows to more than 30 centimetres long.

Giant centipedes hunt mice and birds

33

Birds

Nightingale

Puffin

Hummingbird

Lovebird

Northern cardinal

Stork

Ostrich

Flamingo

Oystercatcher

Blue-footed booby

Canada geese

Raggiana bird
of paradise

African grey
parrot

Barn owl

Peacock

Chicken

Duck

Macaroni
penguin

ALL ABOUT BIRDS

Some birds fly far and high over land and sea and others are fast runners and swift swimmers. There are 10,000 different kinds of bird in the world.

A swallow is an expert flier

Birds are the only animals that have feathers. A bird also has a beak, no teeth, two legs and two wings.

Few animals can travel the world as easily as a bird. By flapping its wings, a bird can take to the air.

Eye

Song thrush

Beak

Wing

Belly

Tail

Feet with claws

Fluffy, warm feathers are called down

Body feathers cover the fluffy down

Long flight feathers grow on the wings

A bird's feathers keep it warm and help it to fly. These are the main types.

Tail feather

A stork's long toes help it to walk across muddy marshes

A duck's webbed feet are like paddles

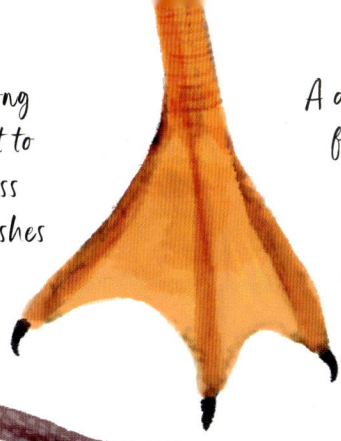

A coot has wide toes for walking on floating leaves

Birds of prey have sharp claws called talons

Ostriches have large padded feet for running

A bird's foot is just right for its way of life. Strong toes and claws help a bird to perch on a branch or to grab on to prey and webbed feet are great for swimming.

A toucan's huge beak can reach fruit at the tips of branches

A bird of prey uses its strong hooked beak to grip small animals

A heron's long, slender beak is perfect for grabbing slippery fish

A bird's beak can tell us a lot about the food it eats. Each is the perfect shape for their favourite type of food.

EGGS AND CHICKS

All birds lay eggs and most birds build nests. Parents take care of their eggs until they hatch. They feed and protect their chicks and teach them how to find their own food.

Female ostrich

Male ostrich

Long-legged ostriches are the tallest birds in the world. They are too big to fly but they can run very fast.

Ostriches live in Africa

A male ostrich has made a nest on the ground and a female has laid her eggs inside. She sits on the eggs to keep them warm, and the male will help out too.

Ostrich egg (15 cm)

Emu egg (13 cm)

Goose egg (9 cm)

Chicken egg (6 cm)

Quail egg (2.5 cm)

Hummingbirds build
the smallest nests

A nest is a safe place for a
bird to keep its eggs. Birds
build cosy nests in branches,
in tree holes, on the side of
cliffs or on the ground.

A swallow's
nest is made
from mud
and spit

A weaver
bird's nest hangs
from a branch

Chicks stay close
for safety

Baby birds learn how
to find food by copying
their parents. Ostriches
eat seeds, flowers,
grass and bugs.

Fluffy ostrich chicks hatch from
their eggs after 40 days, ready
to walk. They leave the nest
within a few days.

A baby bird grows inside
an egg. All the food it needs
is inside it too. Some birds lay
one egg at a time, but quails
lay more than 20!

Newly hatched ostrich
chicks can be as big
as chickens

HUNGRY BIRDS

Birds eat all kinds of food. They don't have teeth, so they usually swallow food whole and then grind it up in their stomachs. Flying and building nests is hard work, so a bird is always hungry!

Gannet

Gannets will fly for hours, searching the sea for any signs of fish. When a gannet spots a meal it dives head first into the water to grab it.

A fresh fish!

A flamingo's feathers turn pink because it eats pink food

A bee-eater catches a flying bug. It throws the bug up in the air and swallows it in one big gulp.

Bee-eaters eat bees and dragonflies

A flamingo eats by hanging its head upside-down in water. It uses its big beak to scoop up water, then it filters out tiny shrimps using its comblike tongue.

Birds of prey hunt animals to eat. They are fast, strong birds that have very good eyesight and large clawed feet called talons. Owls, eagles and falcons are birds of prey.

Barn owl

Soft wing feathers mean an owl can fly silently

A sharp, hooked beak can tear up food easily

This snail kite has caught its dinner. It will use its perfectly hooked bill to pull the snail's soft body out of its shell.

Strong, clawed feet can hold onto wriggly prey

The hoatzin is one of the smelliest birds!

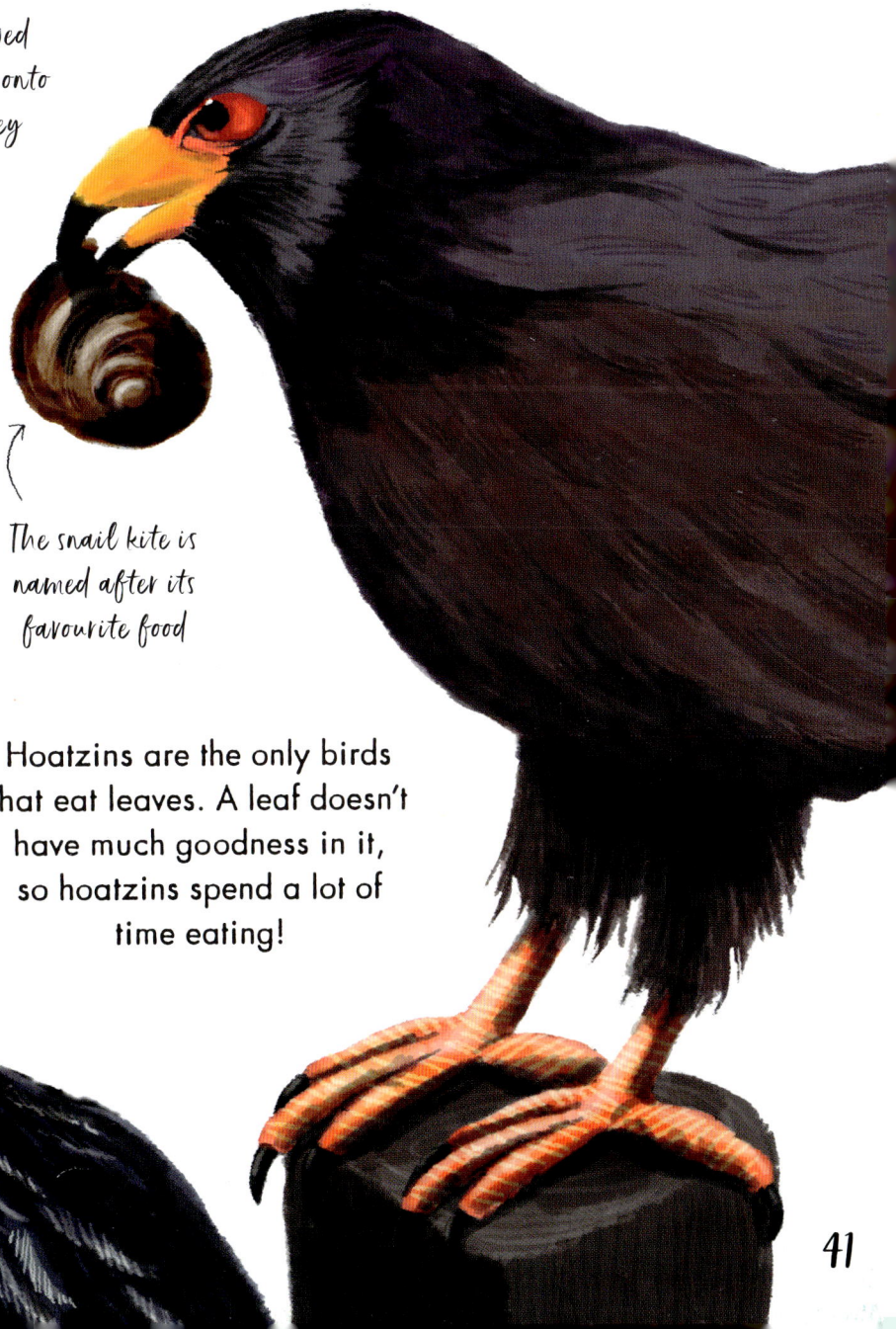

The snail kite is named after its favourite food

Hoatzins are the only birds that eat leaves. A leaf doesn't have much goodness in it, so hoatzins spend a lot of time eating!

PENGUINS

The freezing Antarctic at the South Pole is home to millions of strange birds called penguins. In winter, Emperor penguins gather on the ice to find mates.

Penguins waddle or belly-slide across the ice

APRIL
Winter is coming and the sea is turning to ice. Emperor penguins have been fishing in the sea, but now they swim to land.

Mother birds walk back to the sea to fish while the fathers look after the eggs

Thousands of birds gather in a group called a colony

Father penguin

MAY
A mother penguin lays one egg and the father carefully places it on his feet. His soft belly feathers cover the egg and keep it warm.

There are 17 different types of penguin. The emperor is the biggest. These others live on islands around the Antarctic.

Macaroni

Chinstrap

Gentoo

NOVEMBER
The whole family returns to the sea to enjoy the short Antarctic summer.

Chicks can't swim until their black and white feathers have fully grown

Mother penguin

AUGUST
The mothers return with food for the new chicks. Both parents look after the chick as it grows bigger and stronger.

A fluffy coat of soft, grey feathers helps to keep chicks warm on the ice

JULY
After 70 days the egg hatches. A cold wind blows, bringing blizzards of snow. The fathers and chicks have not eaten for two months.

SONG AND DANCE

Many birds talk to each other by singing. They may also flick their colourful feathers and perform dances to show how they are feeling.

A male nightingale sings a beautiful song to attract a female

Birds make different sounds, from hoots to cheeps and tweets. Baby songbirds start to learn their songs from their parents at just 10 days old.

A male lyrebird sings and shakes its long tail feathers to impress a mate

Bitterns have a loud, deep booming call. Their song can be heard up to 5 kilometres away, making it the loudest bird of all.

African grey parrot

Bittern

African grey parrots are copycats. They mimic the songs of other birds they hear in their rainforest home.

Two cranes perform a bird ballet that can last for hours. The courting pair move together, bowing, leaping and flapping their wings.

Raggiana bird of paradise

Japanese cranes clatter their beaks together

A male blue-footed booby impresses his mate by showing her his lovely blue feet. The bluer they are, the more attractive she thinks he is!

Birds of paradise are the superstars of the bird world. Males have fancy feathers in bright colours and they show them off in dazzling dances.

Blue-footed booby

45

WATER BIRDS

Many types of bird live near water, because there is plenty of food to feast on. Huge seabirds soar over the blue oceans and slender-legged wading birds feed on small animals at the shore.

Heron

Storks find fish, frogs and worms to eat in shallow water

Rivers, lakes and marshes are home to birds with long legs and big feet – just right for wading through water and mud.

The strange-looking shoebill has spied a fish in the murky water

Baby swans are called cygnets

Puffins nest on cliffs, and fly out over the ocean to catch fish

Black-headed gull

Oystercatchers use their pointed beak to pick worms and shellfish from the sand

The shallow water where the sea meets the land is home to many sea creatures, such as fish and crabs, all tempting to hungry waterbirds.

A pelican's huge beak can scoop up a mouthful of fish

Petrel

Birds that live at sea have long, broad wings for soaring over the water – often for weeks at a time. They dive into the water when they spot something to eat.

Albatrosses can glide for hours on their huge wings

Penguins use their flipper-like wings to fly through the water to chase fish

47

Lar gibbon

Giraffe

Warthog

Animals

Ring-tailed lemur

Capybara

Arctic hare

Jerboa

Tiger

Poison dart frog

Red squirrel

Marmot

Rhino

Bat

Lioness
and cubs

Yellow
eyelash
viper

Reindeer

Chameleon

Tapir

Gorilla

Fennec fox

Mouse

HIDE AND SEEK

With no fur or feathers, amphibians and reptiles have slimy or scaly skins. Bright colours and bold patterns help them hide from hungry predators or show off to mates!

A chameleon's long sticky tongue . . .

. . . is perfect for catching flies

Chameleons are lizards, and many are green so they can hide amongst the leaves of their rainforest home. But when they get excited, their skin turns a rainbow of colours!

This amphibian wants to be seen! A poison dart frog's bold colours warn other animals that its slimy skin is covered in poison.

Strawberry poison dart frog

A horned frog looks like a brown leaf on the forest floor, because its colour and body shape help it to blend in. This is called camouflage.

Horned frog

Snakes are reptiles with long bodies that can slither silently to sneak up on prey. Many snakes have a deadly bite, and all swallow their food whole.

This yellow eyelash viper likes to hide amongst bananas

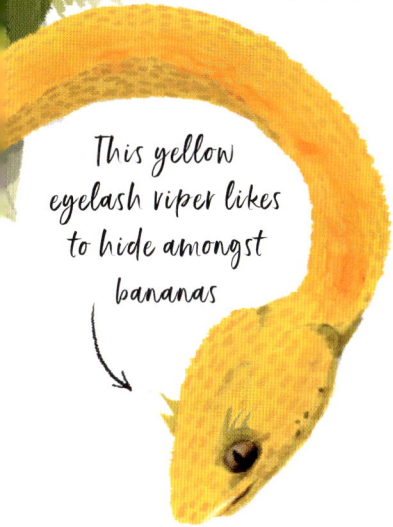

Emerald tree boas are hard to spot in the leaves

Young eastern newts live on land and their skin is bright orange. Adults live in ponds, and turn greeny brown to hide from predators.

Young eastern newt

Crocodile

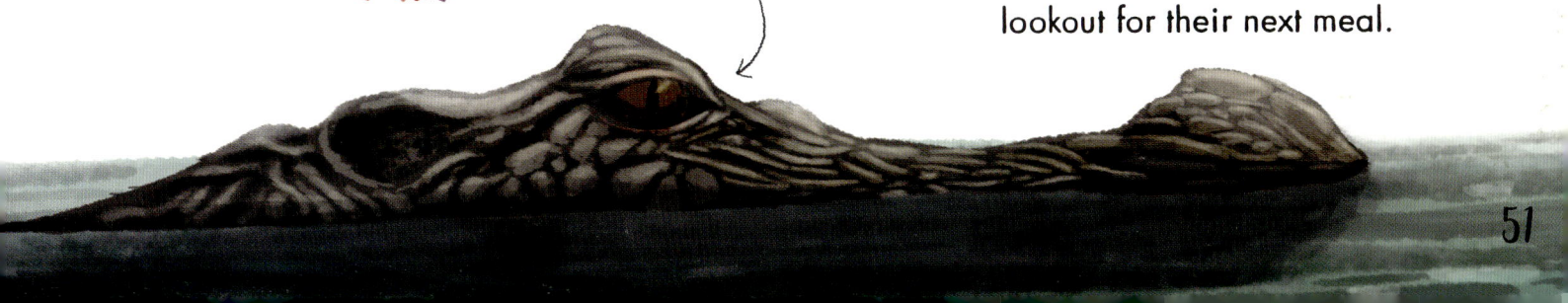

Crocodiles lurk in rivers and swamps. They swim along slowly with just their eyes and nostrils above the water, keeping a lookout for their next meal.

FAMILY LIFE

Monkeys and apes are mammals that are found in forests in warm places. They live in friendly family groups, taking care of each other and looking after the babies.

A spider monkey calls to other monkeys to tell them there's food to eat

Spider monkeys live in big groups. They love hanging from branches and leaping through the trees. Their long, gripping tail helps them to get around.

A male gorilla is called a silverback

Gorillas are the largest apes. They are too heavy to climb trees, so a family builds a soft bed of leaves on the ground.

Lar gibbon

Gibbons have long arms to swing through the trees. At sunrise, males and females call to each other in a chorus of loud hoots.

Mother and father golden lion tamarins take turns to look after their babies. These small monkeys get their name from the fur growing around their faces.

Like all monkeys and apes, tamarins stroke and clean each other's fur

One hundred chimpanzees can be in one family group. These apes eat fruits, nuts and insects, and they have learnt some clever ways to get at them.

Ring-tailed lemurs search on the ground for fruit, leaves and flowers to eat. They hold their tails up high so they can see each other.

Chimps use rocks to crack open tough nuts

Ring-tailed lemurs

53

ANIMAL HOMES

An animal's home is called a habitat. From snow-covered mountaintops to sun-scorched deserts, animals can make a place to live almost anywhere on Earth.

A thick layer of fat helps seals keep warm

Reindeer snuffle in the snow to find plants beneath it

Polar bear

Arctic fox

An Arctic hare's fur turns from brown to white in winter

In the polar lands at the far ends of the Earth, the winter is long and very cold. Many animals have warm white coats that camouflage them.

Mountain goats clamber up and down the steep slopes

Bald eagle

On steep, rocky mountaintops, few trees and plants grow and the weather can change quickly. Animals that live here must be tough and sure-footed.

Alpine marmots live in cosy burrows

A bobcat's spotty coat helps it blend into its rocky home

A desert is a hot, dry place that gets almost no rain. Few plants can grow, but there are some amazing animals that have adapted to survive in the heat.

An Arabian oryx can go without water for weeks

A fennec fox's big ears can hear beetles in the sand

Dromedary camels store water as fat in their hump

Jerboas leap across the hot sand on their kangaroo-like legs

Spotty jaguars prowl and hunt in the leafy shadows

Toucan

Sloths hang from branches all day long

Tropical rainforests are warm and rainy. From the bottom of a river to the tops of the trees, animals find places to hunt, hide and relax.

Tapir

Tapirs and capybaras feed on fruits, shoots and berries, often near water

Capybara

55

THE AFRICAN SAVANNAH

The savannah is a special habitat in Africa where grass grows on vast plains. Herds of grazing animals munch the grass, but there are some hungry predators here, too.

Flying vultures look out for food

Herd of wildebeest

Little rain falls for half the year, so herd animals, such as wildebeest, journey to other places to find water and food. When the rains come again, the grass grows back and the animals return.

Giraffes

Zebra

Hippos

Waterhole

Male lion

Rhino

Lioness and cubs

Gaboon viper

Lions live in family groups called prides. The male looks after his pride and will fight other lions that come close. The lioness does the hunting, so she can feed her cubs when they are hungry.

Dung beetle

A huge grassland is called a savannah in
Africa, a pampas in South America, a prairie
in North America and a steppe in Russia.
Few big trees grow because there is little rain.

Termite
mounds

Herds of antelope
and elephants roam the
grassland. They stay
together for safety while
they graze on plants.

Antelope

Leopard

Elephants

Vultures

Crocodile

Acacia tree

Weaver
bird nest

Weaver bird

Little yellow weaver birds
dart between trees. They
weave their hanging
nests from grass.

Warthog

57

OCEAN WORLD

The underwater habitat that lies beneath the surface of the ocean is home to the largest animal to ever live, millions of fish and lots of other incredible creatures.

Sea grass

Green turtle

Most of the life in the ocean can be found in the shallow, sunlit parts, from corals and turtles, to whales and colourful fish.

Regal angelfish

Huge green turtles come to seagrass meadows to feed. Swaying seagrasses grow in the clear, shallow water at the coast.

Seahorse

Blacktip reef shark

Clownfish

Tiny animals called polyps build rocky reefs. A coral reef is full of food and hiding places, so many animals make it their home.

A coral reef is a rainbow of colour

Red Pacific octopus

Seabirds soar above the waves, watching for fish and jellyfish

Flying fish use their fins like wings to leap out of the water

Dolphins work together to hunt for fish. A group of silvery mackerel dive, twist and turn as they try to escape.

Mackerel

Bottlenose dolphin

The humpback isn't the biggest whale but it can grow longer than a bus!

Mauve stinger jellyfish

Deep-sea vent

Yeti crabs

In the deep, deep sea, there is no sunlight. Steam gushes from deep-sea vents on the seabed, and it turns the water into a boiling bubbly bath for the strange-looking animals that live there.

Anglerfish

Tube worms

IN THE NIGHTTIME

Sleep is important for all animals. Unlike us, many creatures stir at night and rest during the day. Others spend weeks, or even months, fast asleep!

Animals that use the cover of darkness to eat, hunt or find mates are called nocturnal animals.

A barn owl watches silently for mice

Bat

In the day, bats hang upside down in trees or caves. At night, they fly and snatch insects such as moths out of the air.

Cockroach

A red kangaroo grazes at night when it's cool

Tiger

Aardvarks sniff out ants in the dark

Mouse

This red squirrel has stayed up late to collect nuts

Bat

Twinkling fireflies are little bugs that make light in their bottoms. At night they flash to one another through the moonlit forest.

Fireflies

Some animals sleep for many months. In places where winters are long and harsh, some animals would struggle to survive. So they snuggle up in a cosy bed and wait for spring to arrive. A long winter sleep is called hibernation.

Bear and cubs

Some bears, tortoises and rabbits settle down for a deep sleep until spring.

Tortoise

Rabbits come out of their burrows at sunrise and sunset

61

NATURE WORDS

AMPHIBIAN

An animal with slimy, wet skin that can live on land and in water.

BUG

Any small, boneless animal, such as a slug, spider or fly, that lives on land.

CAMOUFLAGE

How some animals blend into their habitat.

DECIDUOUS

A type of tree that drops its leaves each autumn.

EGG

An object laid by female animals, such as birds, that has a baby inside.

EVERGREEN

A type of tree that keeps its leaves all year.

HIBERNATION

A time of long rest during the winter.

INSECT

A small, boneless animal that has six legs and three body segments. Some have wings.

LARVA

A baby insect.

MAMMAL

An animal that normally gives birth to live babies and feeds them with milk.

MATING

When a male and a female meet to make babies.

MOULT

When a bug loses its old skin to grow bigger.

NATURE

All things not made by humans, including plants, animals and the landscape.

NECTAR

A sugary liquid that flowers make.

NOCTURNAL

Animals that sleep in the day and are awake at night.

POLLEN

A yellow dust made by flowers.

PREDATOR

An animal that hunts other animals.

PREY

An animal that is hunted by other animals.

ROOT

Part of a plant that grows in the soil. It collects water for the plant.

REPTILE

Lizards, crocodiles and snakes are reptiles. They have scaly skin.

SEED

Part of a plant that can grow into a new plant.

VENOM

A type of poison made by animals. Some insects and snakes inject it into their prey.

LADYBIRD HUNT

You won't find a ladybird on pages 42–43. These bugs are found all over the world, except the freezing Arctic and Antarctic.

HER MAJESTY QUEEN ELIZABETH

The Queen Mother

AN 85th BIRTHDAY ALBUM

Introduction

OLWEN HEDLEY

'Elizabeth is with us now, perfectly charming, so well brought up and will be a great addition to the family'. So wrote Queen Mary, consort of King George V, on 3 February 1923 after the betrothal had been announced of their second son, Albert Duke of York, to Lady Elizabeth Bowes Lyon.

Queen Mary's words were of almost prophetic vision. On 20 January 1936 King George V died and when, on the following 10 December the new King, Edward VIII, abdicated in preference to renouncing marriage with a divorced American lady, the Duke of York succeeded to the Crown. The abdication had shaken the nation and threatened the monarchy: but the new King and Queen were already popular and, guided by Queen Mary's experience and personal devotion to 'darling Elizabeth', shouldered with exemplary courage the unexpected burden of Sovereignty. The very title chosen by the King gave immediate assurance of his regard for tradition. While to the family he remained affectionately 'Bertie', to his country he became King George VI.

Even before he and his consort had moved from 145 Piccadilly, their London home, into Buckingham Palace, crowds were gathering outside the house to cheer them and their two young daughters, the Princess Elizabeth, now Heiress-Presumptive to the Crown, and the Princess Margaret Rose. And when the Coronation took place in Westminster Abbey on 12 May 1937, the new reign was celebrated by wild demonstrations of affection. The fact that the new Queen Elizabeth was the first consort to come from British stock since the 16th century was in itself an endearment.

As memorable as her own regal attributes and unfailing devotion to the King in public duties is the loving home life she created: nowhere more notably than at their country retreat since 1931, The Royal Lodge in Windsor Great Park, into which they moved during the Second World War. During those years the King, who had served in the Royal Navy and the Royal Navy Air Service in the previous war, 'went to work' each morning, championing the war effort, and with the Queen travelled untold miles to visit bombed areas and victims. 'In the tender smile and comfort of the Queen', declared the Prime Minister, Winston Churchill, 'many an aching heart found solace'.

The strife ended, the tenor of regality was resumed and in 1947 the marriage of the Princess Elizabeth and Prince Philip, Duke of Edinburgh, took place. But grief was to return. On 6 February 1952 King George VI, a sufferer from a lung ailment, died in his sleep. Three veiled queens followed his coffin to its state catafalque in Westminster Hall: the new monarch, Queen Elizabeth II, the widowed consort, who assumed the style Queen Elizabeth the Queen Mother, and Queen Mary.

Queen Elizabeth II was then only 25. Today Her Majesty is a grandmother, and the Queen Mother, after more than 60 years of dedication to her royal role, a great-grandmother, universally loved and honoured.

*   *   *

ABOVE: *Three studies of Lady Elizabeth Bowes Lyon by Samuel Warburton painted in 1923, the year of her marriage to Prince Albert.*

FACING PAGE: *The Queen Mother waves from her balcony at Clarence House on her birthday in 1983.*

Early Years

RACHEL STEWART

Future historians will find no record of the birth of Queen Elizabeth the Queen Mother in the nation's official archives. The reason for this strange omission is that her father, then Lord Glamis (although shortly to succeed as 14th Earl of Strathmore), neglected to register her birth within the required time. Her Majesty was in fact born in London on 4 August 1900 and was christened Elizabeth Angela Marguerite Bowes Lyon.

Lady Elizabeth was born into a large and happy family with seven older brothers and sisters. After the arrival of her younger brother, David, the two became inseparable playmates, affectionately known by their mother as 'my Benjamins' (from the name of Jacob's favourite son in the Old Testament). Elizabeth and her 'darling Bruvver' had an enchanted childhood amid the woods, lawns, flowers, statues and rambling outhouses of their family homes. Although much time was spent at The Bury in the village of St Paul's Walden in Hertfordshire, the ancient Lyon family seat was Glamis Castle in Scotland, a romantic and mysterious setting for the games of two imaginative, fun-loving children.

As she grew older, Elizabeth excelled in the schoolroom under the tuition of her governesses, with history, languages and music her favourite subjects. She passed her Junior Oxford examinations 'with distinction'.

On her fourteenth birthday and as a special treat she was to visit the Coliseum Theatre in London, but her birthday party was overshadowed by the devastating announcement that Britain was at war with Germany. Henceforth Elizabeth's life was to change dramatically; four of her brothers joined the Forces immediately and Glamis Castle became a convalescent home for wounded soldiers. Her sister, Rose, trained as a nurse and quickly took charge of its administration with Elizabeth's help.

*   *   *

THIS PAGE: *Elizabeth Bowes Lyon, aged two in her high chair at St Paul's Walden Bury; Elizabeth and her younger brother David aged four and three; A favourite pastime was dressing up, 1909.*

FACING PAGE: *A watercolour of the lovely eight-year-old Lady Elizabeth, by Mabel E. Hankey; On Bobs, her favourite pony c.1909; Lady Elizabeth in July 1914; Elizabeth's future husband, Prince Albert, aged 19 in the uniform of midshipman of the Royal Navy. He later fought in the Battle of Jutland; Elizabeth and sister Rose welcome a soldier to the convalescent home at Glamis Castle.*

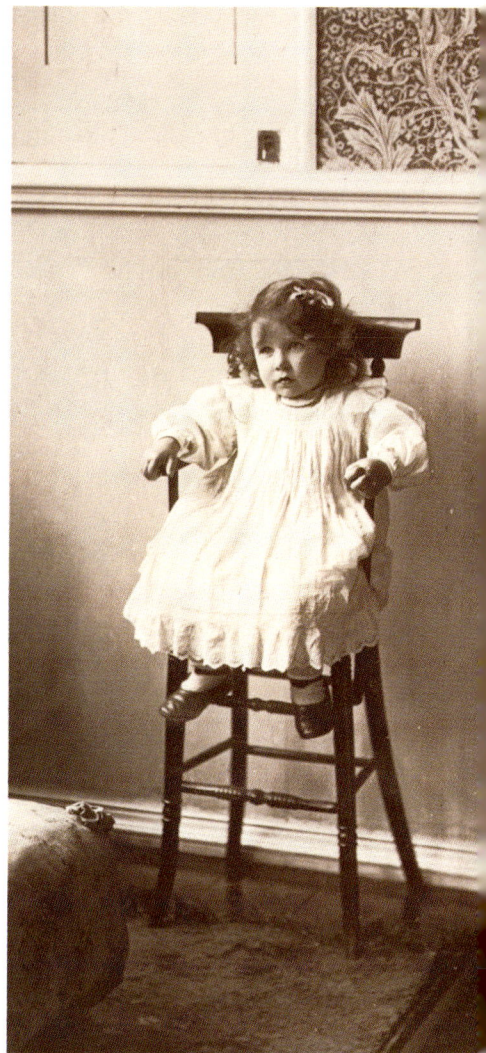

The Twenties

The war dragged on for four desperate years, but happier days were to follow. Peace came in 1918 and Elizabeth was launched into society with her coming-out dance the following year.

Before she was 20 she became District Commissioner of the Girl Guides, and through this appointment she met Princess Mary, daughter of King George V and Queen Mary. They became close friends and Lady Elizabeth was frequently invited to *thés dansants* at Buckingham Palace. However, it was at a dance given by Lord and Lady Farquhar on 20 May 1920 that Prince Albert, second son of the King and Queen, first fell in love with the lively, warm-hearted Elizabeth.

It was a memorable summer for the shy young prince; in June his father created him Duke of York, and in July he proved his prowess at tennis by winning the RAF doubles championships at Wimbledon.

In the following year his romance with Lady Elizabeth developed and he was determined to marry her. He told his father of his intentions. 'You will be a lucky fellow if she accepts you,' was the blunt response. Although very fond of Albert, Elizabeth was hesitant to accept the heavy responsibilities that would fall on her shoulders as a member of the Royal Family. In the kindest possible way, she turned him down, but Albert was not deterred. Encouraged by his mother and sister, he persisted and over the months the relationship gradually blossomed and finally he was accepted.

On 13 January 1923 the King and Queen, who were at Sandringham, received a telegram which said: 'ALL RIGHT – BERTIE.' Three months later, on 26 April, Albert and Elizabeth were married in Westminster Abbey. They were cheered by the crowds, said to number a million, which lined the route of the wedding procession. But times were hard in the aftermath of war and Elizabeth tactfully requested useful, inexpensive presents.

Everyone was delighted with the match. To the public she was 'the smiling Duchess'; the Prince of Wales remarked that she had brought 'a lively and refreshing spirit' to the Royal Family; and one of her own family said, 'Thank God she has married a good man.'

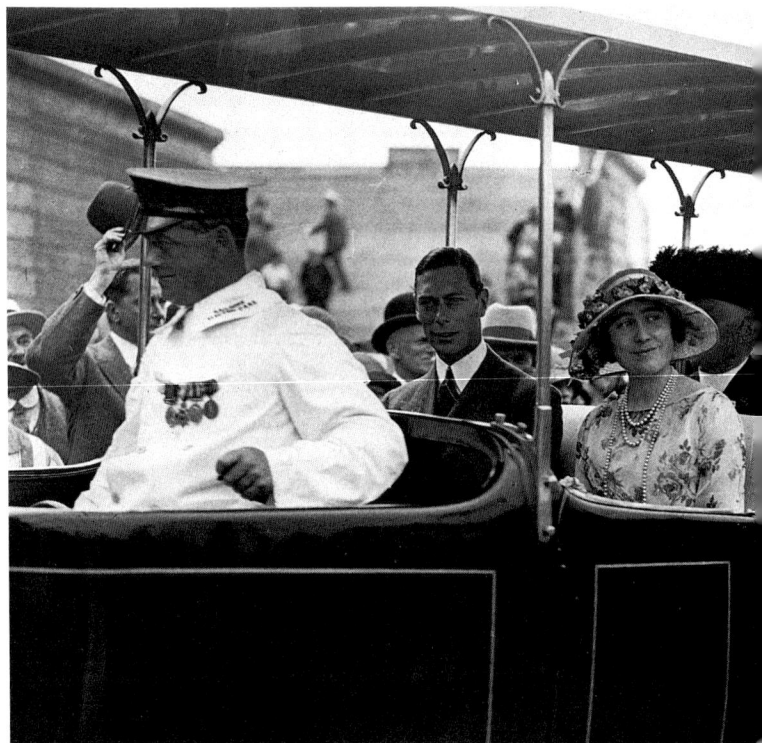

FACING PAGE: *Factory girls in Edinburgh greet the newly engaged couple; The Wedding on 26 April 1923: Lady Elizabeth's dress was made of ivory chiffon moiré embroidered with pearls, and her veil was bordered with rare old lace lent by Queen Mary.*

THIS PAGE: *The Duke and Duchess of York arrive at Ballater station for a holiday at Balmoral; The honeymoon was spent quietly at Polesden Lacey, a country house in Surrey; The Duke and Duchess at the opening of the Wembley Exhibition in 1924.*

7

Although only 23, Elizabeth assumed her duties as a member of the Royal Family with natural ease and grace and became a dedicated partner in her husband's work. Their days became crowded with public duties and, whether it was a great State ceremony or a visit to a Durham coal mine, Elizabeth was always totally involved.

After a short stay at the lovely, but draughty White Lodge in Richmond Park, the Yorks moved temporarily into the Strathmore's London house at 17 Bruton Street. Albert had been brought up in the stiff and formal court of King George V, but now Elizabeth was able to provide the relaxed and loving home that he had been denied. Three months later, on the morning of 21 April 1926, the Duchess was delivered of a baby girl. In a letter to his mother the Duke wrote, 'We always wanted a child to make our happiness complete'. The infant princess was christened Elizabeth Alexandra Mary.

Not long afterwards the Duke and Duchess of York were invited to open the new Australian parliament building in Canberra. They set sail in HMS *Renown* on 6 January 1927, but the prospect of a major royal tour was daunting to both of them: to Elizabeth

because it meant leaving her baby, and to Albert because of a stammer he had suffered from since youth. However, his speech had improved considerably since his marriage, and encouraged by Elizabeth he had consulted a therapist. To his immense relief, he found he was able to deliver his speeches with 'perfect confidence'.

The Australasian tour was a resounding success: the Duchess 'smiled her way straight into the hearts of the people', wrote a Sydney journalist. And there was a poignant moment for Elizabeth in Melbourne with the march-past of ex-servicemen from World War I, some of whom had convalesced at Glamis.

*   *   *

THIS PAGE: *The christening of the future Queen Elizabeth II; The Prince of Wales' farewell kiss for Elizabeth before the Yorks depart for Australia and New Zealand, January 1927.*

FACING PAGE: *In Guide and Scout uniform in Adelaide; An enthusiastic civic reception in the same city; Fishing at Lake Tokaanu, South Island, New Zealand, 1927; Always specially fond of Elizabeth, King George V shares a joke at a charity fete at Balmoral, 1927; With Princess Elizabeth aged three.*

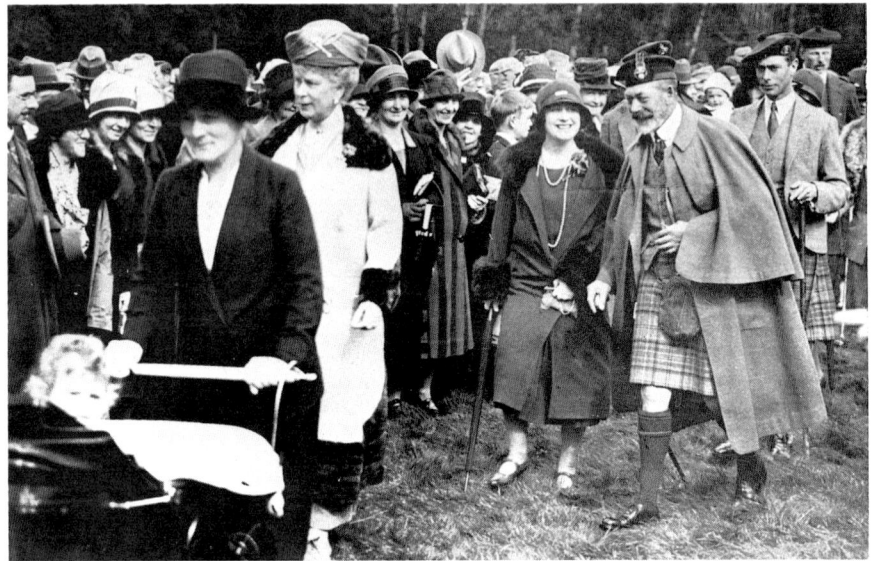

9

The Thirties

The tour of Australia and New Zealand lasted seven months. Re-united with their daughter the York family settled happily into their new home at 145 Piccadilly, and continued the daily round of public duties. In the summer of 1930 it was announced that the Duchess was expecting her second child. Always a Scotswoman at heart, Elizabeth decided to have her baby at Glamis. Her second daughter was born on 21 August 1930 and christened Margaret Rose.

In the early thirties the Duke and Duchess of York, despite their personal contentment, were deeply concerned with the plight of many millions of people in Britain. The country was in the grip of the Depression, there was a great army of unemployed, and austerity was vital if it was to survive. Most families, including the Yorks had to make economies.

In May 1935 the nation celebrated King George's Silver Jubilee. His Majesty's health was failing, but from his room in Buckingham Palace he never forgot to focus his binoculars every morning on 145 Piccadilly where 'sweet little Lilibet' would be waving from her window. On 20 January 1936 the King died, and the Prince of Wales was proclaimed King Edward VIII. His coronation was set for 12 May 1937.

The new reign began with high hopes, for the dashing Prince of Wales had long been a popular figure with the public. But for some time before his father's death he had become romantically involved with a twice-married American lady, Mrs Wallis Simpson, and the King was determined to marry her after she had divorced her current husband. Such a marriage was unthinkable to most of the British people and it was opposed by Queen Mary and other members of the Royal Family, by the Church of England and the Prime Ministers of Britain and the Commonwealth.

The ensuing weeks were exceedingly difficult for the Yorks. The country was in constitutional crisis and the strain on the Duke was particularly intense. On 10 December 1936 King Edward VIII abdicated.

Drawing on her deep faith, Elizabeth wrote to the Archbishop of Canterbury, 'I feel God has enabled us to face the situation calmly.'

The date of the Coronation remained the same, but it was Albert, choosing the style of King George VI, and his consort, Elizabeth, who were crowned in Westminster Abbey.

FACING PAGE: *The Duchess with Princess Margaret Rose at her christening, September 1930; Margaret on the swing with Uncle David Bowes Lyon at The Bury. Her mother and cousin Davina help to push.*

THIS PAGE: *A visit to the Middlesex Hospital, London, 1935; The Duchess inspects a model bust of King Edward VIII at a sale-of-work by war-disabled men at the Imperial Institute; one month later he abdicated; The Coronation Medal, issued in May 1937; Elizabeth is crowned Queen Consort; King George VI and Queen Elizabeth with the Princess Elizabeth and the Princess Margaret photographed at Buckingham Palace after the Coronation ceremony.*

11

In 1938 an important State visit to France had to be postponed because of the death of the Queen's adored mother, Lady Strathmore. When it did take place the gay colours of the Hartnell dresses were replaced by mourning white, but the visit was an immense success. 'Elizabeth rules over two nations', declared the French.

Soon there were rumblings of war in eastern Europe as Hitler's armies marched into Czechoslovakia, and Britain began to rearm. The planned tour of Canada and the United States nevertheless went ahead in the summer of 1939 and the King and Queen covered many thousands of miles, with people crowding along the railway tracks hoping for a glimpse of them. The Americans were dazzled by the lovely 'Fairy Queen'. The tour proved to be crucial in strengthening the alliance between Britain and America during the following years of the war.

★　　　★　　　★

THE PICTURES: *With the Royal Company of Archers, the King's ceremonial bodyguard for Scotland; A moment's relaxation on board during the Royal Tour of Canada and America in 1939; A visit to President Roosevelt's country home, Hyde Park, New York; Canadian Red Indians welcome their King and Queen during the 1939 tour.*

The Forties

After war was declared in September 1939, the faith and courage of the King and Queen inspired a spirit of determination and hope among the people of Britain. With little concern for their own safety, they visited the worst-hit areas during the Blitz – often when houses were still burning – and gave comfort to the suffering and homeless. Once in London there was an air-raid warning and they were rushed into the nearest shelter, much to the astonishment of its Cockney occupants with whom they shared a strong and reviving pot of tea.

Buckingham Palace became a refuge for exiled royal families as European countries fell to Hitler's advancing army. The Palace suffered nine direct hits and the King and Queen narrowly escaped injury on several occasions. Strict economies were observed with food, heat and water – only five inches were allowed in the royal baths.

An invasion became increasingly likely, the Queen's handbag grew in size to accommodate a steel helmet, gas-mask and .38 revolver: 'I shall not go down like the others,' she said.

*   *   *

THE PICTURES: *Making clothes and surgical dressings for the Red Cross, at Buckingham Palace; The Prime Minister, Mr Winston Churchill with the King and Queen inspecting bomb damage at the Palace in September 1940; Encouraging the Land Girls to 'dig for victory', July 1944; Sympathetic words from the Queen for a wounded RAF pilot recovering at Wellhouse Hospital, Barnet.*

Ever anxious to be in the thick of the action, the King was finally allowed to undertake a hazardous trip to North America in 1943 to congratulate the troops on their victories there.

After four dangerous years of war the defeat of the German army was in sight, and the victory in Europe celebrations on 8 May 1945 were ecstatic. In London people jumped into the fountains of Trafalgar Square, and the Royal Family and Mr Winston Churchill, with whom they had become close friends, made eight appearances that day on the balcony at Buckingham Palace. Then came victory over Japan and the tremendous Victory Parade in June the following year.

King George VI had emerged as a greatly loved and respected leader of his people, but he was mentally and physically exhausted.

★   ★   ★

THE PICTURES: *During the war years Queen Elizabeth spent as much time as possible with her two daughters; A charming colour photograph taken at Windsor Castle in July 1941; Victory at last! The Prime Minister and Royal Family acknowledge the cheers of the multitudes at Buckingham Palace; The Royal Navy's contingent at the Victory Parade, June 1946.*

For much of the war, the two princesses had lived within the protective walls of Windsor Castle. Peace brought an end to this isolation and the Queen now organized outings to theatres and held informal gramophone dances at Buckingham Palace. Their handsome cousin, Philip of Greece, who was serving as a lieutenant in the Royal Navy, became a frequent and much welcomed visitor.

It became increasingly clear that Prince Philip and Princess Elizabeth were falling in love, and in the summer of 1946 they became secretly engaged; the King felt that Elizabeth at 20 was too young to marry. In the following year, after the State visit to South Africa during which Their Majesties were accompanied by their two daughters, the King gave his assent and the news was revealed to a delighted British public. The royal wedding on 20 November 1947 was just exactly what was needed to provide a brief escape from the austerities of the postwar years.

This happy occasion was followed by another celebration, in 1948, of the King and Queen's Silver Wedding. Then in November that year there was a new addition to the Royal Family with the birth of Prince Charles. He was to bring great joy to his grandparents, but the King was seriously ill.

* * *

THIS PAGE: *A romantic study of Queen Elizabeth taken by Cecil Beaton in 1949; The King and Queen at home in Buckingham Palace; En route to St Paul's Cathedral for the Thanksgiving Service for 25 years of happy marriage, April 1948.*

FACING PAGE: *After the marriage of the Princess Elizabeth and Lieutenant Philip Mountbatten in Westminster Abbey on 20 November 1947, the formal wedding group; At the distribution of Royal Maundy in 1946; Queen Elizabeth at Prince Charles' christening, December 1948.*

The Fifties

In 1949 King George developed severe arterio sclerosis and an operation was essential to save his right leg. A tour of Australia and New Zealand in that year had to be cancelled with 'profound regret and bitter disappointment'.

His Majesty recovered sufficiently for the opening of the Festival of Britain in 1951, but shortly afterwards the Queen was told by his doctors that he was suffering from cancer and that part of his left lung must be removed. Although realizing that her husband was gravely ill, the Queen never allowed her distress to show.

The King recovered from the operation but he was not well enough to undertake his projected Australasian tour in 1952 and it was decided that the Princess Elizabeth and Prince Philip should go instead. After wishing them Godspeed at London airport at the end of January the King went to Sandringham. On 5 February he tended one of his labradors which had injured a paw. He went to bed and later that night died peacefully in his sleep.

Despite her profound grief, Queen Elizabeth could still find comfort for others. She wrote personally to all those who had been closest to her husband expressing 'gratitude for what had been, rather than distress for what had been lost'. Britain and the Commonwealth went into mourning for the King they had grown to love and respect.

A great consolation to Queen Elizabeth in her bereavement were her two grandchildren, Prince Charles and Princess Anne. A further interest was her new home, the Castle of Mey in the remote north of Scotland, which she bought shortly after the King's death to save it from being pulled down. Not only did she create a delightful home, but she also made the neglected estate into a successful working farm.

*   *   *

THIS PAGE: *A happy picture taken on Prince Charles' third birthday with his sister, Princess Anne, and their fond grandparents, November 1951; A frail King George VI waves farewell to the Princess Elizabeth and Prince Philip, as they depart on their Commonwealth Tour, January 1952; Three queens in mourning: Queen Elizabeth II, Queen Mary and Queen Elizabeth the Queen Mother at the King's funeral.*

FACING PAGE: *At the gates of the Castle of Mey with Honey, a favourite corgi, in 1955; On the balcony at Buckingham Palace as the RAF stage a fly-past on Coronation Day 2 June 1953.*

Everyone admired the Queen Mother's courage in returning to public duties so soon after her husband's death, but as she often told her daughters: 'Work is your *devoir* – the rent you pay for life,' and she has never failed to live up to her own dictum. Three months after the funeral she flew to Fife as Colonel-in-Chief of the Black Watch, to say farewell to the First Battalion of the regiment before they left for the Korean War. She enjoyed dining late into the night in the officers' mess, but was up before five in the morning to see her men march away.

The Coronation of her daughter as Queen Elizabeth II on 2 June 1953 must have brought back moving memories of her own crowning.

After the Coronation, The Queen with Prince Philip embarked on an extended tour of the Commonwealth. She was fortunate to be able to leave her children in the capable hands of her mother. As one of the five Counsellors of State the Queen Mother held investitures at Buckingham Palace and hosted receptions for foreign diplomats at Clarence House.

It was with some apprehension that the Queen Mother accepted an invitation to visit the United States in 1954. She found it hard to believe that the Americans could be interested in 'a middle-aged lady, and a widow at that'. At an official banquet at the Waldorf-Astoria Hotel in New York she was so overcome with nerves that she was unable to eat anything at all. When at last she took off her tiara and sank on to a sofa and consumed a plate of scrambled eggs 'in a lively picnic atmosphere' with her hosts, her nerves suddenly vanished. Thereafter her charisma returned and the Americans flocked to see 'Ma Queen'.

Perhaps the most important public post the Queen Mother accepted in 1955 was that of Chancellor of London University. She filled this office with great distinction for twenty-five years, retiring most reluctantly at 80.

*   *   *

THIS PAGE: *With Pippin at Royal Lodge, 1954; A fervent follower of National Hunt racing, one of the Queen Mother's most successful horses was Double Star seen at Sandown in 1958.*

FACING PAGE: *Masai warriors greet Her Majesty during a tour of Kenya, 1959; Having enjoyed her first helicopter flight, the Queen Mother arrives at Biggin Hill in 1955 to inspect two Squadrons at the RAF station; With her grandchildren in 1954 at Royal Lodge; Making a dazzling appearance with Princess Margaret, at the Royal Opera House, Covent Garden, 1959.*

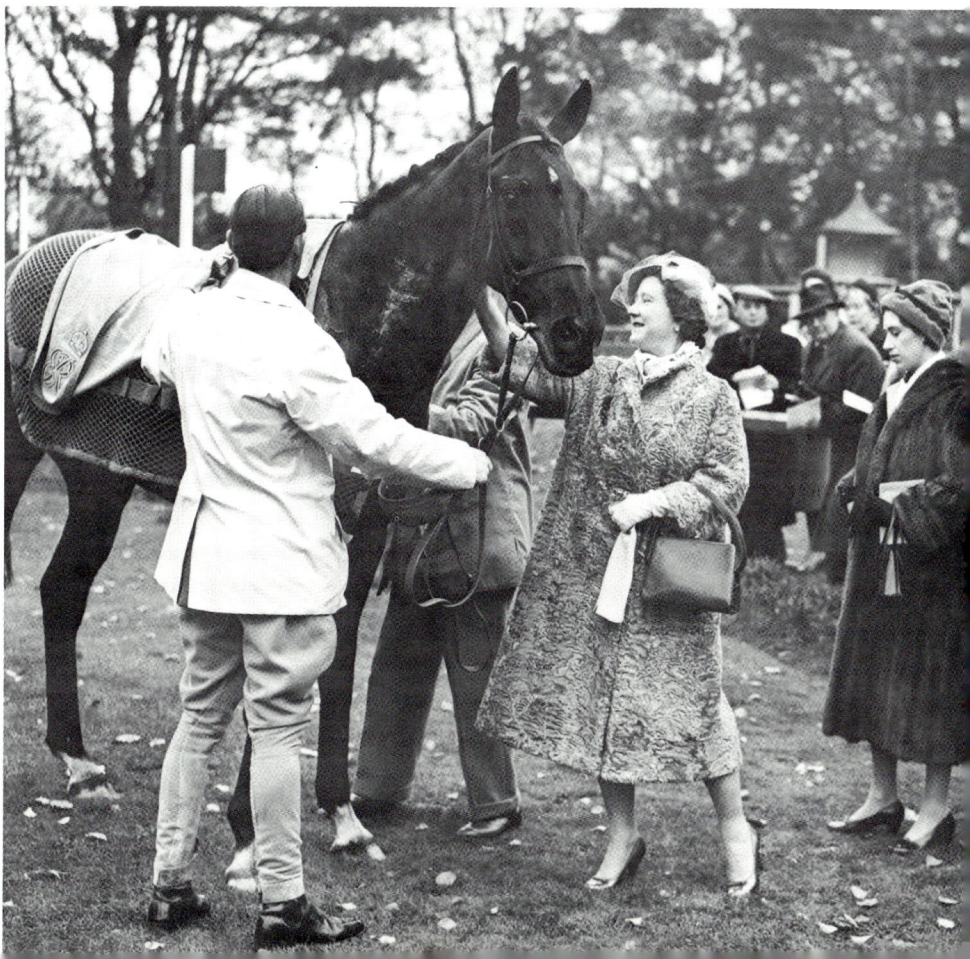

The Sixties

There was much anxiety for the Royal Family when Princess Margaret announced that she wished to marry Group Captain Peter Townsend, a distinguished war hero who had been an equerry to King George VI and Comptroller of the Queen Mother's Household. He was, however, divorced, and Queen Elizabeth II, as head of the Church of England, had been unable to give her consent. There had also been political opposition. During this difficult period, the Queen Mother was always outwardly calm and composed but inwardly all her understanding and love must have been for her daughter.

Towards the end of 1955 Princess Margaret made it known that she accepted that her duty was to sacrifice her marriage plans and to part with Group Captain Townsend. The Queen Mother arranged for the Princess and the Group Captain to meet privately at Clarence House, '. . . and with the most wonderful tact and sweetness she left the room so I could say goodbye,' he recalled many years later.

The sixties were to bring happier days. 'I'm so pleased you are going to marry Margaret,' the Queen Mother told Antony Armstrong-Jones, after he had proposed. 'Ssh,' he whispered, 'I haven't asked The Queen yet'. The Royal consent, however, was granted and well wishers hoped that Princess Margaret had found happiness at last.

Sixty is the age of retirement for most women in Britain, but the Queen Mother at that age was as busy as usual. Exceptional stamina and dedication are required to enjoy 15 different engagements in a 16-hour day. Such routines were, and still are, typical on foreign tours. The inevitable hitches are faced with customary calm. Once the Queen Mother's equerry lost his brief-case containing her next speech, which had to be very hurriedly re-written in the aeroplane. There was no blame; after she delivered it, she said to him, 'I think we did that rather nicely, didn't we?'.

*   *   *

THIS PAGE: *At the Royal Festival Hall, 1962; A 60th birthday picture taken with baby Prince Andrew and his older brother and sister.*

FACING PAGE: *Her Majesty with Princess Margaret on the way to Ascot, 1960; A breeder of cattle herself, the Queen Mother presents a trophy at the Royal Show in Ayrshire, 1960; Knowledgeable discussions with Lord Rosebery and a jockey at Epsom on Derby Day, 1963; Greeting guests at a Buckingham Palace garden party, 1962.*

22

Important annual events which the Queen Mother invariably attends are the ceremony of Trooping the Colour on Horse Guards Parade in London in June to mark The Queen's official birthday; the solemn Remembrance Day service in November, when a member of her Household lays a wreath at the Cenotaph in Whitehall on her behalf for those killed in the two World Wars; and the Order of the Garter Service in St George's Chapel, Windsor Castle, which is usually held in June. The Garter Service holds personal significance for the Queen Mother. The day after the Coronation, King George VI conferred on her this most senior order of chivalry.

Despite her crowded schedule of public engagements the Queen Mother manages to find time for her private pursuits and pastimes. She is passionately fond of National Hunt racing. It is said that she inherited her love of the Turf from her great-uncle, the 12th Earl of Strathmore who was a notable amateur jockey.

The Queen Mother used to make regular visits to the stables at Fairlawne near Tonbridge, where her horses were trained by her friend, Peter Cazalet and she often attended the local meeting at Lingfield Park. It was at Lingfield that she won her first treble with The Rip, Laffy and Double Star.

The sixties saw many racing victories for her until the tragic death of Peter Cazalet. Since then she has owned fewer horses, but by the end of the 1985 season her wins totalled a staggering 351.

Second only to racing, fishing has been a lifelong pastime of the Queen Mother, which she shares with her grandson, the Prince of Wales. In 1966 by a happy coincidence he was spending a few months in Australia at The Geelong Grammar School, Timbertop while she was on a tour of that country. They arranged to meet and spent an idyllic weekend fishing in the River Bend in the Snowy Mountains.

*   *   *

THIS PAGE: *The Queen Mother inspects Chelsea Pensioners on Founder's Day at the Royal Hospital, London, 10 June 1966; A fishing trip to Lake Wanaka, New Zealand, 1966.*

FACING PAGE: *With Princess Margaret and Princess Anne at Trooping the Colour ceremony in 1969; A sprig of shamrock for Fionn, mascot of the Irish Guards, on St Patrick's Day, 1969; On Ladies' Day at Epsom, 1961; The Garter Ceremony, June 1969. Taking part for the first time, Prince Charles accompanies his grandmother.*

24

The Seventies

As the years passed the Queen Mother has inevitably felt the loss of many of her close friends and family. The early death of her brother, David Bowes Lyon, was particularly hard to bear. Another great loss was the death of Lord Mountbatten. The Royal Family were at Balmoral when on 27 August 1979 they received the dreadful news that 'Uncle Dickie' and his grandson Nicholas and a local boy had been killed in Ireland by an IRA bomb. This tragedy brought grief to all the Royal Family.

But there has been consolation in the arrival of grandchildren, and, more recently, great-grandchildren, and she is adored by all of them. The Queen herself has said how 'marvellous' her mother is with the children, 'always standing back and never interfering'.

Many years ago, in an unusually truculent mood, the young Lady Elizabeth Bowes Lyon had written in lieu of an essay: 'Some governesses are nice, others are not'. Times have changed considerably since those days of strict governesses and the Queen Mother has seen her grandchildren grow up in a relaxed and less formal environment. Viscount Linley, Princess Margaret's son, went to a co-educational school instead of the stern Gordonstoun where his older cousins were sent and is now a skilled cabinet-maker, and Lady Sarah, her daughter still lives at Kensington Palace, but rides to art school on her bicycle.

Her Majesty takes her role of grandmother very seriously. Once when The Queen and Prince Philip were away in Australia, someone was heard to remark after a strenuous engagement, 'I hope, Ma'am, you can take it easy tomorrow for a change'. The Queen Mother replied, 'Take it easy – This weekend I have the boys on my hands. I shall probably be playing cricket'.

*　　　*　　　*

THIS PAGE: *The first woman ever to be Lord Warden of the Cinque Ports, the Queen Mother is greeted by cheering children at Dover 1979; As Chancellor of London University, Her Majesty confers doctorates at The Royal Albert Hall in 1972; Three generations of royal ladies, The Queen Mother with Princess Anne and The Queen during the State visit of Queen Juliana of the Netherlands, 1972.*

FACING PAGE: *A windy day at the Castle of Mey, 1976; At Ascot, 1974, accompanied by Princess Anne; Watching the Badminton Horse Trials in 1976, with members of her family and the late Duke of Beaufort; A charming 75th birthday portrait.*

The Eighties

On the morning of 4 August 1980, the crowds were gathering outside Clarence House and sackfuls of cards and presents were arriving from all over the world to wish the much-loved 'Queen Mum' a happy 80th birthday. Soon the Mall was reverberating with the sound of the Welsh Guards playing 'Happy Birthday to You'; the guns at the Tower and in Hyde Park fired their salutes; and vapour trails of the RAF left the letter E inscribed in the sky.

That evening the Queen Mother attended the première of *Rhapsody*, a new ballet choreographed especially for her by Sir Frederick Ashton. A magical moment came during the grand finale when hundreds of silver petals floated down from the ceiling.

Music and the theatre have always given the Queen Mother tremendous pleasure. She is particularly fond of ballet and likes listening to music. At family parties she often sings music-hall songs to the delight of all.

Her Majesty shares her deep love of music with Ruth, Lady Fermoy, her close friend and lady-in-waiting for many years. They were both overjoyed when their grandchildren Prince Charles and Lady Diana Spencer decided to marry. Before the wedding the Queen Mother played a protective role towards the young Lady Diana who stayed with her at Clarence House for a time after the announcement of the engagement to escape the harassment of the Press. The bride-to-be also spent the night before her wedding with the Queen Mother and they sat together in front of the television watching the firework display in Hyde Park. The Queen Mother had hurt her leg, and there were fears that she would be unable to attend the wedding, but nothing could possibly prevent her. It was a radiant grandmother who drove in the triumphal procession to St Paul's Cathedral with the bridegroom's brother and supporter, Prince Edward, at her side.

*   *   *

THIS PAGE: *On her 80th birthday, the Queen Mother acknowledging the cheers of the crowd at Clarence House. With her are The Queen and Princess Margaret, Viscount Linley, Prince Edward and Prince Charles; With Ruth, Lady Fermoy in King's Lynn.*

FACING PAGE: *In reflective mood, September 1982; A local event near the Castle of Mey, the opening of the Canisbay and District Royal British Legion Hall; A brisk walk on a Norfolk beach; On the balcony at Buckingham Palace after the wedding of the Prince and Princess of Wales, 29 July 1981.*

Although her role of Queen Mother involves her in all the great matters of State and its ceremonies and pageantry, Her Majesty is by no means cut off from the rough edges of day-to-day life in Britain. After the serious riots in Brixton in 1981 she was one of the first public figures to visit the devastated area. Her presence did much to restore calm.

A year later Britain was at war with Argentina over the Falkland Islands. The Queen Mother's grandson, Prince Andrew, was serving in the aircraft carrier HMS *Invincible* as a helicopter pilot and was in the thick of the action. Those were anxious days for members of his family but the Prince survived unscathed. In June, the Queen Mother embarked in HM Yacht Britannia and welcomed in the Solent the QE2 returning home with the survivors of ships sunk in the South Atlantic.

For a lady who is well into her eighties the Queen Mother is remarkably fit. One of her favourite ways of unwinding and taking exercise is to walk with her pet corgis. Apart from a serious operation in 1966, she has only suffered the odd twisted ankle, and the incident in 1982 when a fish bone lodged in her throat which had to be removed in hospital. This she described as the 'salmon's revenge'. Even on unpleasant occasions her sense of humour never seems to desert her.

For an octogenarian, her list of engagements is simply staggering. In 1980 she made ten journeys overseas, took part in 63 ceremonies, officiated at four investitures and held 14 audiences. In 1983 the number of public appearances rose to 117 although she paid fewer visits abroad. She is patron of 300 organizations, among them the British Red Cross Society, Dr Barnardo's Homes, the Girl Guides Association, the Royal Horticultural Society and the National Trust. She is also Colonel-in-Chief of eight British regiments and Commandant-in-Chief of three women's services, not to mention her office as Lord Warden and Admiral of the Cinque Ports and Constable of Dover Castle.

*　　　*　　　*

THIS PAGE: *In stunning yellow: a charming study made in 1982; With the Irish Guards after the presentation of shamrock on St Patrick's Day, 1984 in West Germany.*

FACING PAGE: *Snooker at the Jersey youth centre, 1984; The children of Sark greet the 'Queen Mum' with flowers; Feeding the pigeons in St Mark's Square in Venice during the visit to Italy; The Queen Mother is said to love flying in helicopters: alighting in Sark, 1984.*

A glance at the Court Circular gives a fair idea of the hectic pace of the Queen Mother's life – scarcely a day goes by without mention of her presence at some important function. On 17 March 1983, for instance, she was in West Germany attending the Irish Guards' St Patrick's Day Parade; on 21 March she was at a royal film première for charity; on 22 March she helped entertain the President of Zambia at a State banquet; on 24 March she was at the Annual General Meeting of Queen Mary's London Needlework Guild, followed by another official banquet at Claridges . . . and so on.

Some years ago it was suggested that Her Majesty might become Governor General of Australia or of Canada, but The Queen was adamant: 'We can't do without her here'. There is no doubt that her vast experience of public life is invaluable to other members of the family who constantly seek her advice.

Perhaps the key to this amazing energy and dedication to duty lies in her enjoyment of it all. For, as she has said herself on many occasions, it is all 'such fun'.

     ★   ★   ★

THE PICTURES: *The Queen Mother's fourth great-grandchild, Prince Henry, was christened at Windsor, 1984; A time to remember – at the service in Westminster Abbey on the 40th Anniversary of VE Day, May 1985; At the film première of* A Passage to India, *1985, with the Princess Anne and the Princess of Wales.*